Basset Retri
20 Milestone Ch

C000151799

Basset Retriever Memorable Moments. Includes Milestones for Memories, Gifts, Grooming, Socialization & Training

Volume 2

Todays Doggy

Copyright © 2019

Dedicated To All of You Wonderful Owners and Fans

Under Control

I've Got It All...

For MY Bedtime Story

I'm Ready

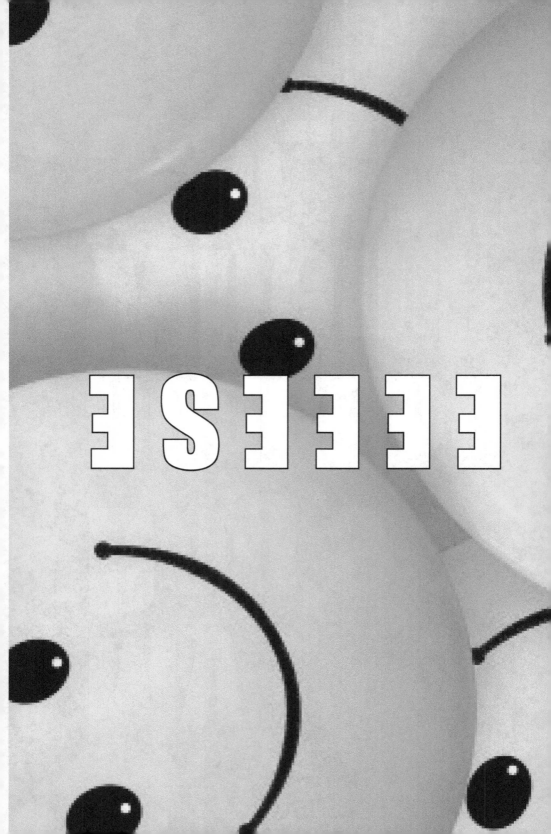

I'm

Always

Listening

Your Secrets Are Safe With Me

I'm Sleeping

see

can

AS you

I Wonder Who Did It!?

OH LOOK!

Someone Has Made a Mess!

I'm Just On

Energy Saving Mode

I'm Not Lazy

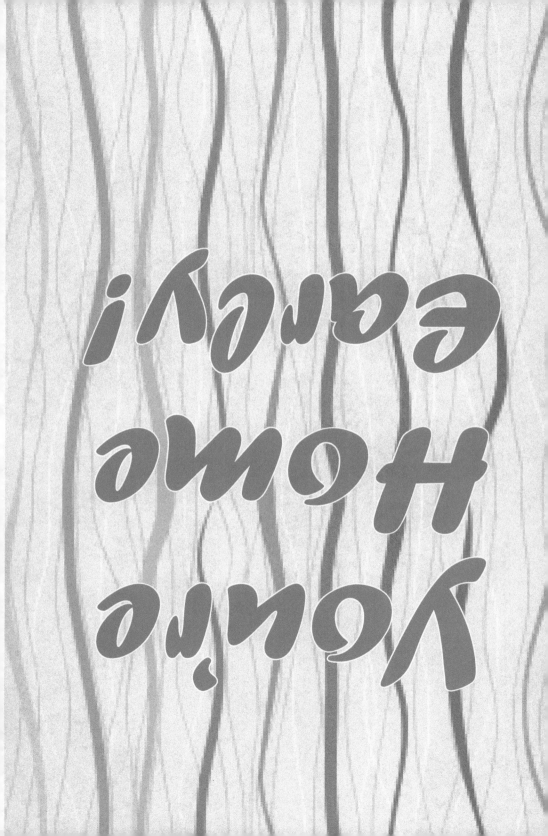

The Joys of Being Groomed

Ahh...

iEven know how TO High 5

I'm SO GREAT

Who's The Doggiest Of Them All?

MIRROR MIRROR ON THE WALL...

AND
SOMEONE KNOCKS ON THE DOOR...

WHEN YOU'RE HOME ALONE

What I'm Doing

I Have No Idea

Was a "RUFF!" Day

"Bad... To The Bone

I'M
BBBAD

Too Busy to Talk!

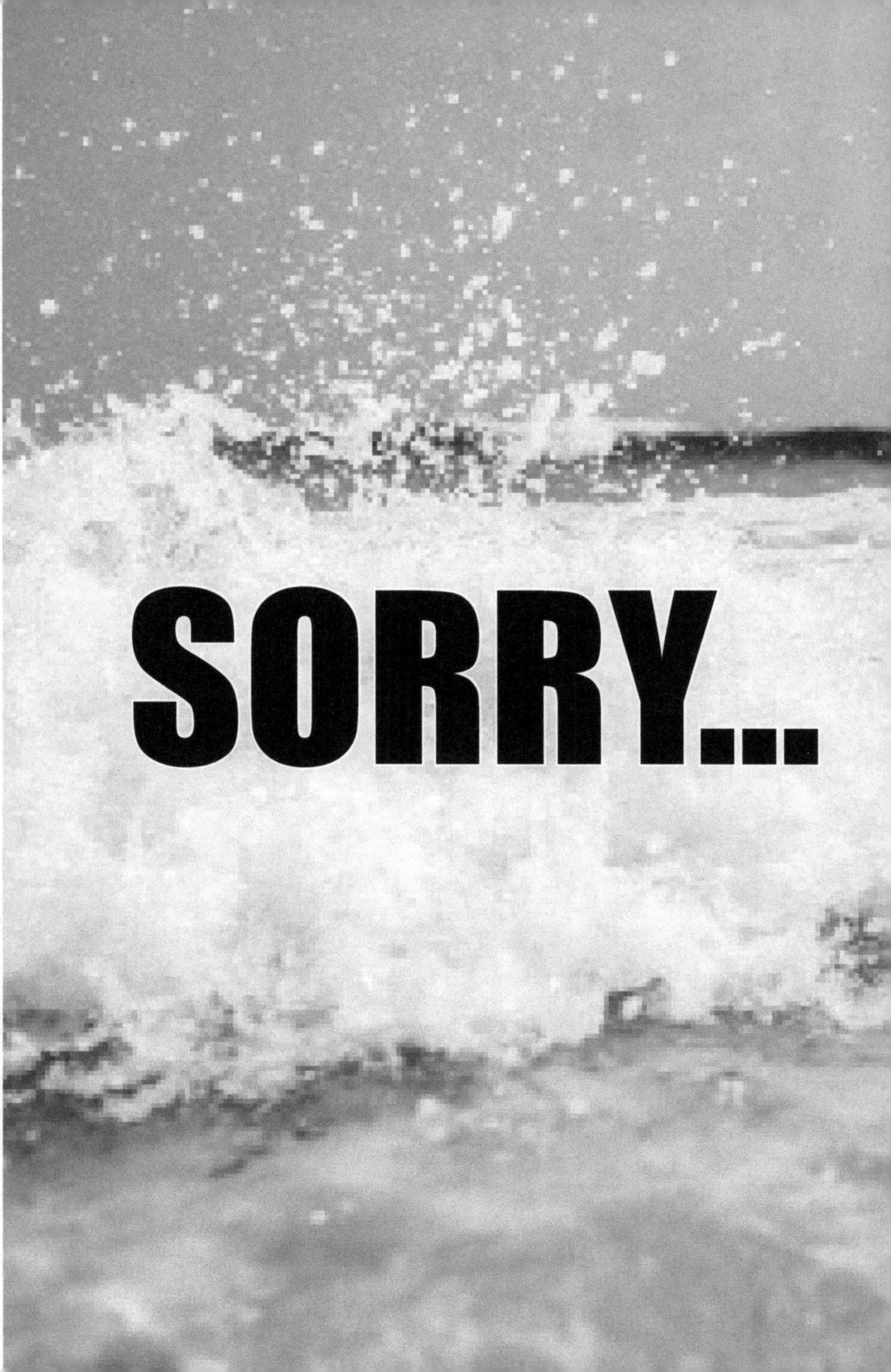
SORRY...

Who Wants To Hear It?

...Don't I?

I Look Rather Fetching

So I Helped You Finish The Food

I Noticed You Were Sleeping...

Introduction

Welcome to the Original Doggy Milestone Series™ where you are encouraged to create those special moments with your dog. We have composed the milestones in a way that challenges you to set the stage before taking your photos.

Use props and make it fun - be creative in setting up your photos. Get family and friends involved - take it out with you - use it in different places and settings - have a play with it and most importantly, have a good time!

You can either hold the desired milestone spread open yourself - or have somebody hold it open as you take the snap.

If you would like to have the selected milestone book spread open and standing independently in your photos, you can use one or two large 'foldback' clips to hold the spread open.

Share your photos with friends, family, and communities - look for feedback and areas of improvements in order to create even better memorable photos.

Good luck and enjoy your photo fun.

CPSIA information can be obtained
at www.ICGtesting.com
Printed in the USA
BVHW060210140919
558390BV00008B/660/P

9 781395 336967